TRACE ELEMENTS

Nigel Forde was born in Leeds in 1944 and currently lives in York. He spent many years working as a professional actor before turning to writing, and has since written several poetry collections, plays for the theatre and radio, and four novels.

Nigel has won several poetry prizes and is a longstanding tutor for The Poetry School. He has also written for and performed with several theatre companies, including Riding Lights Theatre Company, which he co-founded.

Previous poetry publications include *Teaching the Wind Plurals* (Robson Books, 1991), *A Motley Wisdom* (Hodder & Stoughton, 1995), *A Map of the Territory* (Carcanet OxfordPoets, 2003) and *The Choir Outing* (Carcanet OxfordPoets, 2010).

Trace Elements

N‍IGEL F‍ORDE

Valley Press

First published in 2018 by Valley Press
Woodend, The Crescent, Scarborough, YO11 2PW
www.valleypressuk.com

First edition, first printing (March 2018)

ISBN 978-1-908853-91-2
Cat. no. VP0108

A CIP record for this book is available from the British Library.

Cover design by Fitzpatrick Designs. Text design by Sasha Hawkes.
Edited by Martha Sprackland.

Printed and bound in Great Britain by
Imprint Digital, Upton Pyne, Exeter.

Contents

i.m. John Bailey

The Forge

What I wanted was the blackbird that tipped
His short-score from my great-aunt's lilac
And the swan she said had sat for Bewick;

The mattress of leaf-mould where we walked the dog
In underwater light, and the way September
Dealt with sun, with distances. In the forge

I watched him bring the dead to life: the metal
From the tractor's saddle, shares and shears,
Chain, blade and chassis. Out it came, not yet

Living, but promising life, like breath from a lung,
And he stroked it out of fire into the midnight folk
Whose lives he knew: owl and fox, otter and heron.

More real than the real thing, people said. It was
My first lesson in metaphor, the truthful lie;
The way to keep all light, all blackbirds, swans.

Near Triscombe Stone

Exmoor is where distances paint out
   Kale-coloured hills and wash them
Into pea-green or lime, resolve the bilberries
   Through grey and purple back again to blue.
Whatever prediction we attempt
   Dissolves in rising light, in statements
Of what must be and what may be there.
   The clouds unpick themselves
To a blue they have remembered
   From the blue that gathered round Venus
Hanging, heavy, in a swarm of stars.
   The dogs snuff up what night has hidden,
Untussock fox and rabbit scent, are ripples
   In fathoms of bracken. Our eyes grip nothing,
Tangled in a counterpoint of here and there.
   Our feet crumble the hoofprints on the track
And away in a darker green the stream
   Crumples over softening stone, looking
For a level which it never finds and from which
   We climb away into a newborn sun;
Heather ticks on shoulder blades of stone,
   The oaks hang like bells, and the air
Is all appetite where ravens slide,
   Where invisible stonechats fire
Tiny gunshots from gorse, from bilberry and thorn.

Riding a Bicycle

for George

The soundless collisions stagger the trees,
The sullen sky withholds its rain, and you're
On this implausible geometry.

First there was walking. Done. Then
There were words. Then ways to manage
Love and absences. Easy for you now.

But this is an instinct, unteachable,
And if you get it wrong the tarmac
Bites, the hedge has claws.

We take it in turns to pant beside
Each lurch, each wobble, ready to
Bring up ointment, an ambulance.

We lie to you: 'Go on, I've got you!'
But we haven't. And it doesn't matter:
Suddenly the sky is wide and clear,

The black path is a red carpet rolled out
For you, VIP, champion, unwitting master
Of Newtonian physics.

You pose for photographs,
Accept our tributes, then off you swoop again,
Eyes fixed, head down,

Delighting in our delight
And – small genius – in the dusk
Scribble your nonchalant fugues all the way home.

The Truth

Endeavour looks always towards perfection. The utterly
Finished. Full stop. The everything-in-its-place finality.
Outside is nothing but strive, strive and sway

Above the hedgerow's green glut: that imponderable
Where we can never arrive; where everything is awry,
Untidy, making the best of, and failing again and again.

We are left in a gulp of night air, in the encompassing dark,
To be alone. Alone, then, we make music –
Shapes, to pull the world out of and into orbit, to parse

Sentences of the heart, search impossibilities, wanting,
Wanting always, and finding no answers but the beauty
Of the flawed. A viol roughs out only a fair translation,

A sackbut cannot tune the chord, a treble falters
In the cathedral, flutters, bird-like, on the top note.
So we affirm the truth of music. Not perfection:
Only uncertainty. The frangible, wounded, human.

Les Baricades Misterieuses

Crocus. Hellebore. Osmanthus. The garden murmurs
Only quotations; the full text still to be published.
Birds on the telephone wires are unidentifiable.
They huddle together like cold clergy.

Light is an essay; tries to explain a thesis
But gropes for meaning, makes do with mere rhetoric.
It is most acute when least apparent, when
Midday whispers to the ice-thin lightless moon.

A moment, and every shape knows its own importance.
A harvest of place, an accomplishment of colour,
A patter of twigs. Couperin from the radio,
Discourses of silence where every sound matters.

Measuring

i.m. Norman MacCaig

The world exists in language
But doesn't have one.
So if I want to listen to it,
Talk to it, play Kim's game
With what it's keeping from me
On its bright, baffling tray,
There's one-fag you;
Always you,
And your lexicons of perfect imprecision.

Kinderszenen

PRUE

Another day explaining the treble clef.
First the spaces: F, A, C, E;
The lines – after me: E, G, B, D, F.

She once played Prokofiev and Chopin
For Menuhin's sister at a charity concert in Bath,
As if the children would know, their parents be impressed.

The tinies' fingers can barely stretch a fourth;
They pay the bills, that's something.
But *Fairy Revels* and *All A-Twinkle* can give way
To *Träumerei* and *Bittendes Kind* at four o'clock
When Richard comes from school,
Smelling of blazer and pencil-shavings.

She has taught him the flat keys: Flats Become Easier
After Direct Guidance. Believes he may remember
The sharp keys: Go Down And Enter By Force;
That's the mnemonic for majors.

Five to four. A crunch on the path. A shadow
In the mirror. A touch of lipstick, powder.

First, Richard, warm your hands. We'll work today
On touch. Warm yet? Between your thighs
Is best. She demonstrates. Fingers must be flexible.
Stroke, like this; press gently, like this. Don't rush.

Sometimes his hand slips. Sometimes hers.
Sometimes there is laughter. There are often long silences.

Every Good Boy Deserves Favours.
Remember that, and in the next lesson – *Glückes Genug* –
We'll push on; see if I can take you
Through the relation between minor and major.

JOHNNY

He takes a packed lunch in his army satchel,
A scotch egg, a tomato and a bottle of cider;
Goes where the field fries with grasshoppers
Like the silence between his temples,
Where there are no women among the trees
Or spread on the hot bracken; where nothing
Needs to be listened to or understood;
Only the sparrowhawk with murder in its eyes.

PALMER

Only comes out after dark.
Has a pond of paint water marbled with scum
That, like him, never sees the daylight;
Under its lid, below the spongy branches,
Newts ripple, frog spawn thickens.

A grey house, foursquare, flat and vile
Sags above it like a wall eye.

There's another at the window.

God may well forgive us our trespasses;
Not Palmer. He'll have revenge.
His pantry is stacked with rank
On rank of tins in case of another war.
It's declared on Friday when we boys come.

A jam jar starts it, glinting in the sun.
The eye gleams back.
Enemy approaching. Into action.
The window opens and the air hums, whistles
With pilchards, corned beef, sardines, Spam,
Soup, baked beans, pineapple, mandarins.
We grab what we can and run.

No tadpoles but we save on coupons.

MELANIE

'There's nothing to be afraid of,' she heard,
And believed it as her belt snapped off, as the breeze
Caressed her stomach, as her ear pressed
On the buckle of her school bag. It was a game.
It was not blood, she thought, but elderberry juice.

Under another elder, in a sweat of leaves, a fox;
The muzzle was black with blood, blue with flies
And maggots were boiling in its belly. She had
The smell by heart and the prickle of leaves.

Black pearls, an Arthur Rackham woodland
For *Beauty and the Beast*, the light foundering,
The dark reaching for another chapter of the story.

Now she cannot take the quick way home,
Never able to banish quite the knowledge

Of the terrible things that happen under elders.

JIM

A village of good things. Kind people
Busy behind windows in steam and light,
In the clink of cups and plates,
In the soft noise of fires burning.

Of all good things nightfall is what we love.
We inhabit twilight; they will bend with us,
Loose us, give us huge permissions.

But this is a midnight and he has loomed in it:
The mythical but always-possible, the icy blade,
The other side lurker between here and home,
The horror, the appalling uncle of a tombstone.

Here is a stink of mouse cages and sweat
From whoever it is – in his flare-path
Of red lanterns and paraffin pleating the road –
Who leans over the brazier and blows it
To a blue bat-ear of flame.
He has a name but tonight we cannot find it.

Hideous. His eyes gone; Rembrandt-pits
Of darkness, ellipses of nothing,
Black Os; he swings his skull like a snake, flickering,
Skin drawn tight and orange leaping in it.

A car goes by whose headlights fray
In what will soon be fog. He turns to it.
He has a face again and passes us his tin.
'Roll us a fag, mates, you can have some tea.'

BERTRAM

Helped home again and left in the dark
By the cold fireplace, the foxed mirror,
He leans against the mantelpiece and dribbles;
Bellows at headlights that reel a slither of windows
Across the ceiling-spin until the neighbours
Thump another flake of plaster from the walls.

The light has gone on the stairs. The sink
Is larded, the scrap-bucket crawls. A bath tap drips.
There is the smell of dog but the dog has gone.

Another night of hurling photographs and weeping,
Another slump into clammy oblivion
And the taste of heartbreak. Down the road
The Home Service is being cheerful
To comfortable couples fenced with flowered curtains.

MARY

It's slovenly to leave the candlesticks where they were
Last night. The words in the Readers' Letters
Must be counted and filed. There's a code somewhere.
A correlation. It will come.

She opens all the cupboard doors upstairs
And downstairs to let things out; boils a kettle
For breakfast. When she's collected twenty packets
She's allowed to start on the cornflakes. Not long now.

She speaks on a walrus cough of indrawn breath. Four
People in the village can understand. Others cross
The road on remembered errands. She likes
Children: they are always laughing, always laughing.

The parcel needs refreshing. Wednesday was the ashtray
From Littlehampton and Thursday was the toasting fork;
Today, a pack of coal or Blunden's poems? Coal
Is good company, and the watering-can is hard to wrap.

Bad mistake yesterday. Today both shoes are on.

These trees are not quite right; not quite the ones
In the picture over the fireplace. But they'll do.
Her hair spreads on murmuring leaves. Thrushes
Are in the orchestra, her parcel is tucked
Into her side. Here, nobody complains, gets ill,
Nobody dies, nobody misunderstands.

And there are children in the distance. She likes
Children: they are always laughing, always laughing.

PHIL

More grief than the house can bear
Sends him out to drown in the Milky Way.
All beauty falters even in spring's inventions.
Unreasonable questions are squeezed out of the silence:
Why this mantelpiece? Why the mirror?
What meaning can remain
In books, in curling photographs?

He tries the impossible: looks forward
To yesterday, fills empty pockets
With anniversaries and dust, the trivia,
The stupid, intimate trivia of delight.

The skin itches under his wedding ring
Pale, shrivelled, always out of the sun.

RODNEY

He required a sop, like Cerberus.
Spangles or a cigarette. He'd make do
With a swig of your Tizer on a good day.

He'd stand waiting with his door wide open,
Wreathed in sweat and 'Music While You Work'
To which his jaw, cheeks and forehead
Kept a sort of time. Always in horrible motion.

And he'd be there even if you went
The long way round by Clammer Hill
And down to Prestwick Lane.
Unable to read or write, slow of speech,
He seemed to have the gift of prescience
And endless appetite. Smugglers always failed,
Came home with bruises.

No one ever told us where he went.
We didn't ask. Things happen. One day
The door was closed, the house
Silent. His mother became a regular at evensong
And wept at the prayers for the sick.

Harry

Rictus. A face of winespill. A scrawled
Relief map. One milky eye, one crater.
His village green is a boiling oil-slicked sea
Where children cling to wreckage, where
Cottage chimneys make smoke full ahead
And gulls scream 'Dive! Dive!' and the shop bell
Pings like radar. Whose stillness is terror,
Whose soft smile cannot leak, closed behind scabs,
Sewn into speechlessness.

CHARLIE

He likes frills. He longs for Aertex, lace and cotton;
Touches them in fabric shops but never buys,
Only looks, remembers,
And then hobbles away.

The lovely journey is into the woods. An hour
Is not too long to wait, lips tight as a purse,
For Susan or Dinah who sometimes creep
Away from games because they have to.

Susan has her delicate way of looking
Right and left and right again, as if
There might be traffic. Then the swift hoist
And crumple of blue skirt, the flick
Of white down to the knee. The tiny
Bottom on a tremble of stalk.

Dinah listens, which makes it difficult to breathe,
But then she's slow; luxuriates in the breeze
On egg-brown legs, and sometimes drops
Her pants beside her on the moss. He loves
The long sigh as she empties, the pause
Before she dips her feet back in her clothes.

He'll store that rustle and snap for his dreams
And she'll walk back unhurriedly, untouched.

Ralph

Discovered his dark one night of frost.
Clung to it. Came out fighting. Shouted
'Hoo-Hoo!' at roads and walls.

Burned lino at new moon. Ate stolen jam.
Painted his kitchen purple. Called himself Ivanhoe
At weekends.

Shot crows, pigeons, larks. Stamped on mice.
Howled at the besiegers who muttered, whispered
From the wireless.

Broke his own windows. Drowned kittens. Knew
The earth one day would reach for him,
Pull him under.

Played Bach's final partita, beautifully,
On his father's violin. Went out.
Laid himself face down in the stream.

KEN

Had a brother, once: the sawmill screamed at him
And he screamed at the dust he soaked into.

A son, once: David Bernard Timothy Malcolm.
In a heavy khaki plane they brought home
Only David Bernard covered in a Union Jack.

A wife, once: her shell sits in the sun on June days
By a lichen-scuffed wall and stares at striped grass,
Topiary, women in white.

In the garden he watches tomatoes, spinach, beans,
Waiting for rot, for blight.

FRANK

Big fish. Came late to our little pond.
Brylcreem. Paisley cravat. Signet ring.
He lopped branches, grubbed up trees;
Stole our pirate galleon, our Texas plains,
Our moated castle, for a kitchenette.
Parked his Lagonda where the tractors turned.

Talked 'Thrift' and 'Endeavour' to the village school,
Joined committees, the crowd at the bar;
A useful second wicket down he said
With his modest and popular smile.
Paid for the Christmas party. Crooned
'Silent Night' through beer fumes and feedback.

Then a ringing more exciting than sleigh bells:
The four black Wolsleys, headlights blazing,
Roaring up the hill at dawn and blocking
The drive to his deserted house.

KAREL

There has been hot metal and electricity
In darkened rooms half-lit by snow
Beyond the grating. Now he has no nails,
Leaps into the hedge and whacks his head,
Howls and slaps himself, spits consonants,
Throws shovels, picks and mattocks from his barrow.

Pity was hinted at, but we understood
Only our fear; dared to laugh at it and him
In safe, sociable chorus by the fire,
Eating our toast, reading Arthur Mee
And the brothers Grimm who'd got him to a T.

He could do things to your eyes, your teeth;
He knew Trolls and Ogres; lived under the bridge
Up to his bum in cold, green water; ate leeches,
Toads, as well as boys; had limbs like us
But bit on the Marsh Monster's language.
Sometimes he wore the grasshopper's
Savage, metalled face.

A night wind could rustle him up from ditches,
And (accustomed to finding 'Rupert's friends
Hidden in the picture') we saw
His unskinned head in every knuckle of the nightwood.
Copses crawled with corpses and with him.

Coming one morning from the farm
He met me, loomed at me from nowhere.
I stood, brave as a bagpipe, shouting silent terror.

His unrepulsive arms jerked, stammered:
'Lovely' – pointing to the sky, his lovely,
Lonely eyes softened with tears – 'Oh, lovely,
Lovely, lovely!'

Beyond Question

You are looking beyond the window for Easter perhaps,
Seeing the crisp surplices, the boiled-sweet glow
Of stained glass and the fat hedgerows singing.

For Christmas and the slump of snow, the scarves,
The torches and the white walk under trees,
Under the million stars.

For harvest time; the bake of stubble
And the flash of rabbits sprayed by the ocean-roar
Of the combine. Gunshots and dust and thistle-sting.

It's all there, painted over the urban clutter that is
There as well if only time would make up its mind
And tell you how old you are, how young.

Matter has mattered for long enough. Now it is only
Impedimenta: you abide in memory's antimatter
Where we were but cannot come again. It is a kind

Of generosity that lets you live with all you love
And where you want to be. You say my name
As if you pointed at a photograph, and sit;

On your knee, our cat who died in 1952
And, on the Light Programme, Secombe, Sellers, Milligan.

Trace Elements

Your gestures have not changed, your voice is still your own.
Your memory may be unreachable
But it goes all the way down; down
Through the dry hours that won't be swallowed.

Everything is unfastened, the glue no longer sticks
Or the tube is blocked, pick at it as we may.
Your magnets are set north pole to north,
And repel a lifetime's filings.

When you can find nothing to talk about,
When yesterday and the day before have deserted,
I want to read you the fields you worked in,
The woods you loved, in and out of season;
The wet nose of the wobbling calf, and hay
Tossed beyond the spill of the hurricane-lamp
Into the raftered dark. Blackberries at the Stroud,
Beech mast crunching underfoot like frost,
And bees stammering in the rosemary.

I can write you into your right mind,
Where choir men cross the green for evensong,
Where Hubert has painted blue poplars
On the outside lavatory door, and there's the 4-shaped
Tree on the top of Hurt Hill, and cheese
Left out for us when rehearsal's over.

Listen. I can write these things and keep on writing.
On and on and on. These sentences
Are where you are alive. You can stay
As long as you need. You're safe here.

Close-up

First a buzzard. Now it's you I am watching
Through binoculars. I can blur you and focus on
The aspen poplars smoking into the smoke-grey
Of Wold-breath and the chestnut horsehead fields;
Or I can foreground you against a swim of ragwort
Hogweed, nettles. Here you come, there you go,
A ghost again at a touch, at the turn of the screw.

I can sharpen the tip of the buzzard's wing
To eyelash, to comb, to saw, then back
To a speck that's caught in a plughole of slow sky.
So many ways of knowing at a distance.

But when you leave your spade and stretch
And stroll towards me, touch the crumpled magenta
Of tiny rose leaves, you fool my mechanics;
Shape-drifting at every step until you are
A smudge, abstract; mere mass of pigment,
Impossible to define; unknowable, except
As simple sunlight scattered into the house.

Crab Apple

Frost-etched and scarred, for years it has been
An unperturbed asymmetry; a frame
For Leo and Andromeda, a choir-stall
For tiny virtuosi. Lean the axe and saw
Against the trunk; climb the ladder. Then pause:
See a new half-inch begin the journey into blossom.

Boutell's Heraldry

i.m. Ward Needham

A madeleine for some, a red-green skirt of evening sky
For others. An interval is idly pressed on the keyboard,
A drawer opens on the scent of boot-polish,
And there's a whisper from the once upon a time.

I open *Boutell's Heraldry* and feel a scored desk-lid
Under my fingers, hear the flump of a muddy football
On a sixth-form boot, see green matchboard and cream walls
Hung with the cast of all the plays you had produced.

As I read the words you taught us, taste their flavour, the rich
Chaucerian otherness of them – gules, sable, tenné;
The metals and the furs, the caltrap, mullet, flanches,
And the crosses – moline, potent, pommé, bottony –

You lean to me in your chalk-dusted gown and together
We trail our clue through a labyrinth to the still centre
Where Latin, maths, mythology, geography, art, music
Hang inseparably alive in the experience of language.

It was your prophecy: how one things leads, if you allow it,
To another and another, how plural are our singulars,
How nothing, except in heraldry, can be an *ordinary*.
You spilled the world over us and we didn't drown.

Years later sitting on your back step, sejant regardant,
We talked like equals, drank tea together
For the first time, and then you pulled from a pocket
A tiny autograph book and passed it to me.

('He's never parted from it,' said your wife.) It was signed
By your Drama Society, one page each. Christina Rich,
Ros Jewett, Vivien Hiscott, Celia Gates, Nigel Forde
And others. Only I don't make my Ns like that anymore.

Oil on Canvas

A message came this morning from the Prince;
It was carried by one of those pomander-danglers
With a sneer, a sword and a horse that will have cost
More than my wages for three years. He came
Rattling up the stairs in spurs, the idiot.
And as he stood perspiring at the door
My portrait of the Duke of Ferrara was
Reflected in tiny detail in the rowels.

Well. It seems I have another mistress to paint
And lice to kill before she dainties in
With some zoo animal in petticoats
As chaperone; some Gorgon who will sniff
A quasi-aristocratic sniff and bridle
At every attempt I make to find out what –
If anything – hides inside those silks and brocades.
Not literally, of course: such expensive flesh
Is not for viewing by an oily-fingered,
Scratch-bearded wretch with nothing much to offer
But a certain skill that, snake-like, must be charmed
Every day, every hour. It can snuff itself out
Like a wetted bonfire and there's no guarantee
It will ever return, though a commission
Is of some assistance, concentrates
What you might call 'the gift'. Who calls it a gift?
The Prince, because to think of it as such
Keeps me below the salt. It's hardly work –
That's the unspoken thought – not tax-collecting,
Building aqueducts or owning land;

No, more like a birthmark or a tendency
To baldness: something quaint and, on occasion,
Amusing. And his mistresses, my sitters,
Drift in, do nothing, and suppose I'm loafing
Like them for those three hours.
                                    There was one –
I have the sketches somewhere – not the usual
Aristocratic ice floe, before whom
I am mere furniture, but a peasant beauty
Straight from the tavern; she (she said) expected
Something more *classical* for her Prince to ogle,
And while I was snapping charcoal, rustled out
Of her bric-a-brac and leaned stark naked
At the window, on tiptoe, buttocks tight
And a tiny furry diamond of Tuscan light
Between her thighs.
                        That's what I sketched:
Her bending, then dipping fingers in my bowls,
Grinding the pestle, sniffing brushes, chalks,
Prodding the stuffed rabbit that does duty for
Ferret, cat, goldfinch, all those creatures
That haven't the patience even of the sitter
But are demanded.
                        The finished picture showed
Her dressed in robes, ultramarine and ermine,
And her hair netted in gold. She didn't last.
So the portrait was sent back. There was no fee.
I was paid, you might say, by the sitter, and the lice
I have to eradicate are hers.

                    I am no more
Than a tradesman: an artgrocer, a portraitmonger,
Fulfilling orders and delivering sweets.
                                        All this
Pays for olives, prosciutto, bread
And the sleep of a troubled conscience. What I mean
Is...What do I mean? That I'm no genius,
But may have something in me which my Prince,
By his generous commissions, by his fondness
For the peachy skins I hide (but hint at)
Under brushwork, is locking up with ducats
In a safe prison.
                        Strange, for when I paint,
There is no safety – only a will, a hunger
To be a door for the impossible,
To haunt heart, eyes and dreams; to spell out light
And all its local dialects, to trap
The fugitive, to be an echo of all
That's noiseless, to plumb a world that has
No ocean floor.
                        Being, though,
Happens in a different world; a world
Of chairs and wine, mirrors and petticoats,
Pine-trees, lutes and icicles. I pillage one
To phrase the muteness of the other. Sometimes
Hours go by in which I sit and fill
With a lonely wind that comes from neither world.

I ask whose is the gift? What shall I do?

Soon there will be a creak on the stairs. A Maria
Or a Rosina or a disguised Marchesa
Will drop, quite unobtrusively, a small
Bag of coins somewhere on the table
And that's my future. Take it and I'll live.
Or so I say.
                    A courtyard clap of hooves.
The rumble of wheels. Then silence. I lift my brush
Then put it down. Then wipe it on a rag.
I walk along the floor, turn and walk back.
One more. I'll do one more: this one. And then.

Droppings

There were always apples, like fires in the grass,
Smouldering in a cap of flies; plums, split
And dribbling sap, while wasps purred and hummed

Like a combine harvester, and the pheasants
Creaked along the hawthorn hedge. There was
Enough for everybody, for mildew and rot as well.

But it never mattered who took what.
Leaves fell along with fruit and we stared
At the steel-gleam of birds hammering with hunger

And thought we heard the clatter of beaks, as a whole
Autumn fell to scuffle and head-jerk. Nowadays
There are still apples and crabs, plums and sloes,

A damp confetti-scatter of ripeness and fermentation
With a reek of cellars and a slow fizz almost heard
Between the stab and whip of beak on soft flesh.

Now we understand and welcome all-comers to drink
The sweat of windfalls, the sun-warmed flesh; and nod
At the clack clack of their scissors snipping in the dusk.

Primer

You learn a landscape word by word, slowly
Over years; grow into it as you grow
Into speech. You pick up its declensions,
Conjugations, by instinct, repetition.
This makes it hard to teach.

The rambling grammar of overgrown paths,
The careless syntax of copse and cow pasture,
Tree, stream and that subordinate clause
(The rutted, potholed track, that goes
Verblessly, gloriously to nowhere)
Will have to be made safe, cut back.
We should lose those tautological beeches, sycamores,
And all the indirect objects that shade the lane;
That purple patch, the blackberry field,
The confusing punctuation where the tractor shed once stood.

We inherited this history of wilderness;
But each month edges back the chance of reading
The dialect, tracing the etymologies.

This fresh print has fixed the language now,
And any liar can learn a language
And speak it faultlessly, quite unlike a native.

Interior. The Studio. Night.

For Chris and Hubert

Look left: you were in Widow Twankey's Launderette.
Look right and there was *Another part of the Forest*.
Against the wall leaned sunlit shop-fronts, a market-place,
The Tower of London, a seashore. I could walk
Through a vicarage study to Versailles or Venice
To Belgravia, Hampton Court or Dunsinane.

Even the police admired your kind of forgery;
They sloped in with a whip of frost during the small hours
And dared to drink the tea you boiled beside the pot
Of stinking size, the treacly fish-glue. They sat
Astonished as I was, by the meaningless
Swash and buckle your quick arm-swerve dashed
Onto the sagging canvas; a careless swoop
Of mere mud-spatter which, from twelve steps back,
Made perfect sense: swung and settled (there should
Have been a chord of music) into rockface or wood-beam
Or creeper or curtain-fold or light on water.

Yours was the wizards' way of working always after dark,
The flagstones oyster-coloured with the splash
From Rattigan, Barrie, Shakespeare, Ayckbourn,
While potent mixtures spluttered on the gas-ring.

You had your mystic runes, your hieroglyphs: OP 2,
DSL, →Kit, PS Transf. The last, one fragment
Of a magic spell that showed Sinbad drifting down
To the slow seabed among a hundred glowing fishes.
I watched you flick and spray and paint
And suck your pipes as I mixed colours
Or charcoaled your perspectives with a strip
Of paint-stained deal. Mostly I primed new canvas
Or flatted-in, blanketing some glory in a slosh of blue.

I can't use colour now; I go for the black
And white of words, and remember the rule you taught
Over the size-pot, among the bags of powder,
As we waited for a wood near Athens to dry;
That in nature nothing is ever truly black;
Nothing is unmixed white.

One Day

Sunshine like an insult. The water makes
Its watery sounds without a pause. The buses run
And children skip and scatter in the playground.

Silent as U-boats the hearses slide
Up to the wall. For an hour, black-jacketed men
Talk low, smoke furtively. Rachel carries out

The tiny chalice full of a dust that knew
Dovetail jointing, watercolour, Latin,
Thomas Tallis, astrophysics, heraldry
And the name of every wild flower.

Poet

For Anne Stevenson

The world is rich, and it mooches around,
Hands in its pockets.

It drops loose change without noticing.
And you pick it up, coin by coin,
Spread it out gleaming on page
After page in front of us, the impoverished,
Who long to be millionaires
Like you.

Night Fall

The sound of night is this: the fall of rain
From loaded gutters, clopping like a horse
That's freed into the yard before the birds have sewn
Their glitter on the Rembrandt sulk of not quite dawn;

A local spring of dirty foam and moss and skeleton leaves,
Last year's footnotes, the old ghosts of winter
That walk in step with me as I lean towards sleep,
Hoping for a clean slate, some sort of banishment.

A Day in October

It is as quiet as homesickness. The body
Sheeted, clean, looking younger. 'They always do,'
The man said. Death is not disturbing,
And at the same time it is. Terribly strange.
One last kiss from the sister who loved him, and I
Make wishes but don't know what they are.

We shall get used to it; month after month,
Men and women going somewhere
All alone and never saying goodbye.
All the fear I never felt
Hovers like a question; but I don't ask.
We go out among the blackbirds, under the sun,

That blazes with no sense of decorum.
What else is there to do but carry on being alive,
And warm and sensible and able to remember?
We must shop, phone, cook, wash and drive,
We must become used to ourselves, ready always
To love and stroke the faces of the dead.

Letters from the Mad Musician

The Mad Musician Surveys His Territory

Unfinished work on the floor, on the far table,
Fragments of song, splinters of sonata. Not a bust
Of Bach or Brahms in sight. I know my place,
And cheap alabaster won't rack it up a single notch.

If I had a dog I'd take him for a walk. Instead
I sigh, just to prove to myself that I'm grappling
With something worth the grapple. It doesn't work.

Nose down over the manuscript paper. Scratch, scratch.
The piano is tempting me, but I'll listen to my headful
Of orchestra, the tang of oboes, the violas' silk,
And the bassoon – voice of the oak tree. One lamp
But two shadows: the second comes from the moon
And the moon is what I am trying to write.

The Effect of Surrealism on the Mad Musician

I am writing a quartet for coffee filter, bonfire,
Ordnance Survey Map and Logarithm Tables.
Could you remind me, dear friend: is the coffee filter
A transposing instrument?

Dilemma of the Mad Musician

My head is full of brass and voices where Stravinsky
And Gabrieli shake down flights of angels; the growl
Of Beethoven in two of his tempers; the stones
At the bottom of Mozart's unruffled lake and the beret,
Rakish, that hides the yearning in the head of Poulenc.

I've had enough of bar-lines, semiquavers, noise;
I want to write the silent music of the nothing doing.

The Mad Musician and Metaphysics

Expanses and abstractions. The unintelligible.
Shapes and the length of shapes. There are
Inventions somewhere beyond joy or sorrow,
But I am afraid, I am very afraid, that they are unreachable
And that if ever they were reached they would be meaningless.
What can I do next?

Sadness of the Mad Musician

I stand at the end of the Pier of Possibility
And into the Sea of Inspiration I cast
My baited Line of Technical Expertise.
I hook out a supermarket trolley.

The Mad Musician Takes a Holiday

I am thinking of taking up painting. Yesterday, as I sucked
A stick of rock, I watched the fishermen smoking
And laughing on the quayside. It was slippery
And silver with scales. The homophone
Did not escape me (nothing obvious passes me by):
Scales, the bones of music, practised
In a dark room with one bar of the heater glowing,
Chilly, lonely, a far cry from this wind-washed sparkle.

I went to a gallery where men and women walked
Past picture after picture with hardly a glance
At all those distillations, all those pleas
To see and understand, to remember and be changed.
I wanted, to my surprise, a prelude, a passacaglia,
A fugue, a loud, loud fugue:
Something that could not be ignored.

I was not fashioned for the open-air life,
Nor am I now thinking of taking up painting. But
I shall have to find more ways of being unhappy.

Epigrams of the Mad Musician

The singing man may have a shop in his throat
But today is early closing.
Consider the semibreve before it considers you.
Music may be the brandy of the damned
But Mahler is the calvados of those still awaiting judgment.

.

Dreadful Birthday Card Verses of the Mad Musician

I reach into silence
For what lies behind;
The press of the moment,
The shape of the mind,

The leaf and the pebble,
The intake of breath,
The time of your life
The sharpness of death.

They're all in this music
I wrote out of you:
'Prelude and Fugue
Opus 9 No. 2.'

The Mad Musician Goes for a Pint

My beer needs its glass, but music simply is;
It can do without my brain. I'm a hunter,
That's all, a stalker; but one who can never see
The quarry, and has no dogs to sniff it out.

What I can do is put these fields,
That grope of woodland, one or two
Constellations into my pocket,
Take them home, explode them

Into abstraction, uninvent shapes, colours,
Into cadences longed for and obvious;
Make a place we feel the need to go to,
And wonder how it was done, who did it.

The Mad Musician Gives a Sigh

I am pulled by this string quartet
Into absolutes of introspection,
Helped to understand what understanding is.

The much-too-charming woman on Radio 3
Speaks of its beauty, but she has a trite
Beholder's eye and the dreadful need
To smile and be accessible.
The music is simple satisfaction, necessity,
Like the behaviour of characters in fiction:
Form, doing what it must. It is
Eternity crushed into twenty minutes
And remaining eternal.

I make a pact with my listeners:
I will tell you nothing and I won't be told.

Musings of the Mad Musician

There are conditions attached
To the receiving of a gift.
One is to know the difference
Between the imagination
And a figment of the imagination.

I make these journeys
And, every time, come home to myself.
A cold coming, and a long trudge
Full of vanishings, full
Of the memorable but unremembered.
Whenever there's a whisper
It seems always to be Honegger
Or Bartók seen through a curtain.
Sometimes I am only what I have learned;
Born at the wrong time
With an appetite
For what's been on the menu far too long.

The Mad Musician Defends Neo-Classicism

I shore up another day by thinking of the dead,
Picking up their threads, following their methods

Whose clarity of purpose, whose stringency, I know
I lack and need to make this more than exercise.

This backward leaning may be dangerous; tends to close off
Certain sorts (uncertain sorts) of fresh neural activity,

Can make me a frame for an alien landscape, for a portrait
Of some fat and forgotten burgher, long dead. But then

I remember *Dumbarton Oaks* or the *Suite Française*
And the fortuitous anthems when Athlone or Hilversum

Creeps through the dark into the glowing valves
Of my antique radio; and I remember the grand

Shog given to the cool dude turning up a trilobite
Just a hundred yards from arcade, chip shop, candyfloss.

The Mad Musician Rolls a Few Names Round His Tongue

Did you ever hear of a composer called Brown?
Or Smerthwaite, Donaldson, Cholmondley? Anything
You'd find in a telephone directory?

Alternatively, where have all the Elgars gone?
Can you find a Bax, Delius, Holst, Vaughan Williams
Who will deliver your coal, plumb in your washing machine
Or landscape your garden? Is there a Dowland
Down your street?

Read the world news in your newspaper,
Inspect even the sports pages full of foreigners:
You'll find no Couperin, Rameau, Vivaldi,
Prokofiev, Mendelssohn, Copland or Beethoven.

All I'm saying is, if you haven't got an unusual name,
Well – it's a worry.

Apology of the Mad Musician

I'm so sorry: I have such cold fingers
I can hardly write. Nor dare I take too much time
Away from my scores, though I have a mission
To save the world from unnecessary tedium
And am deleting from all opera summaries
The phrase 'He falls in love with a young
Gypsy girl, but she…' Also 'The Duke enters, disguised.'

I know you read five books at once; I used to admire that,
But now I have found myself writing five,
Six, seven pieces all at the same time and I run
From table to table, scribbling, jotting, striking out.
I am exhausted but feel inexhaustible. Where does it
All come from? Don't ask, don't ask.
It may never happen again. Is it any good?
Will anyone listen to it?
I'm so sorry: I have such cold fingers.

Thirteen Ways of Looking at The Mad Musician

Through the bottom of three wine glasses,
Through the bottom of two Guinness glasses,
Through the bottom of five whisky glasses,
Through rose-tinted spectacles,
Through the prism of history,
Through the window when he's not there.

The Mad Musician Applies for a Residency

Sir (or Madam if that 'h' was an 'a')
I have written a concerto that is inaudible
Except to dogs and bats. It won a prize
At Lausanne in 2002 but has since been banned
By the RSPCA.

Following the example of Purcell, I am at work
On a Fantasia on One Note. I haven't found
The right note, and when I have I doubt if I shall
Fall into the obvious trap of embellishing it.

I enclose a page of blank paper. This is very similar
To the one I am working on at the moment.
I hope you find something there to interest you.

Owing to prior commitments, were I to be offered
The post, I should not be able to take it up.

The Mad Musician Searches for Inspiration

The harmonics of the wind are too like 'Francesca
Da Rimini' and there's Debussy forever ghosting
Along the seashore. The council hedge-trimmer
Plays Vivaldi all down the road. Holst comes out
At night and Bax follows me through the silent woods,
Messiaen through the noisy ones. I'll try
Bald-headed men, dispirited booksellers, sweet pancakes
And maybe some lingerie.

The Mad Musician Questions his Vocation

I'm not invoking posterity here, not thinking
About 'my legacy' or anything quite so arrogant,
But I constantly remind myself that what I do
Is meaningless: its effects contingent on digestion,
Architecture, memory, temperature, the biographies
Of hundreds, of thousands I have never met.

Every so seldom I write something I think good,
That transmits some kind of meaning,
But I can never prove it. A minim has no etymology,
Nobody can conjugate the semiquaver.
Despite my beautiful calligraphy
Music is an acoustic art. All is in the ear of the beholder,
And that ear may be full of wax or cotton wool
Or palm-court trios playing arrangements of Suppé
And Kreisler in spa towns. Or Dépêche Mode.
I can't evoke woodsmoke, starlight, Tuesday,
Global warming, disinfectant or a mulberry tree;
I can't even manage a meringue.

Don't come talking to me about 'emotion' or 'expression'
Or anything you feel like pasting over my abstractions.
If you happen to meet yourself in my symphony,
That is your business. Keep it so.

I won't reach for the clichés that have become convention:
I write my shapes on the air. Just a child with a sparkler.

The Mad Musician Has a Break

This morning I listened to Palestrina.
There has to be less to life than this.

The Mad Musician Looks through his Photograph Album

That's me with my new bucket and spade;
Hayling Island. These three from graduation day.
And she – she was going to be
My wife, but in the end married a man
With a pension. Look, these are the good ones:

You can't quite see me there, but I'm on the
Third desk: that's my bow. That's me
With Raymond Leppard, and that's me (I had
A beard for a short time) at Wigmore Hall
With Robert Simpson and Rubbra. No,
That's the caretaker but he does look
A bit like Stravinsky.

From the left this one goes Tippett, Rostropovich,
Felicity Lott, me, Alexander Goehr and Mackerras.

That really is Stravinsky. A studio shot. And that
says 'With admiration and thanks for all you taught me. Igor'
Actually I wrote that on myself.

Daydreams of the Mad Musician

A cabin – given free by an American heiress –
Beside a lake where I can write a suite
For strings, a viola concerto and a piano quintet.
The perfect place for a secret affair
With Natalie Dessay or Victoria Mullova.

A commission from the Proms or the Edinburgh Festival.
A choral and orchestral piece, perhaps. Something
For Leif Ove Andsnes? For The Nash Ensemble?

An invitation to Andreas Scholl's birthday party
Where I would give him my present: three cantatas
And a set of songs.

Anyway.
I've got this thing to write for the Flexiglass advert.

The Mad Musician's Disappointment

There are five telephone wires that go from pole to pole
Alongside my garden. Swallows sit on them; sometimes
A rook perches like a tenor clef. There's an idea, I thought.
I brought out the manuscript paper,
Scribbled down what I saw.
I got the Overture to 'Prince Igor'.

The Mad Musician Asks Himself Hard Questions

What am I doing? Last night I walked
In the garden where a tiny rustle
Exploded into a frog. Now it's gone.
Just an incident, over and done with.
But where do noises go?
Do they ever run out of whatever they are made of?

I invent them and arrange them; I've never wondered
Where they put themselves. Did my frog-rustle
(And does my distinctive use of woodwind)
Speed like a bee or float like a dandelion seed
Over fields, saplings, churches, roads, whole villages,
Whole counties, to become at last
Part of the Universe's Complete Catalogue of Sounds?

Is there, somewhere,
The very first performance of K482, or *Le Sacre*
Lurching from constellation to constellation?
Or has it faded until it is no more? Well, then –
What does *no more* mean?

The Big Bang still hangs, they say, in telescopes;
And all my little ones? All of them?
I can't bear the responsibility.

The Ten Commandments of the Mad Musician

Thou shalt neither scream nor mutter but speak.
Thou shalt remember that every day has an umbilical cord.
In travail shalt thou bring forth.
Thou shalt notice not the greenness of the grass beyond the fence.
Thou shalt not measure thyself against the contemporary.
Given the choice between novelty and authenticity,
Thou shalt choose authenticity.
Thou shalt not neglect the impossible.
Thou shalt neither court nor expect applause.
Thou shalt bother. I mean *really* bother.
Thou shalt not be contented.

The Mad Musician is Slightly Disturbed by Time

I shut the study door. Click.
Millions upon millions of years
Of survival and death, of passion and sterility,
Of the unfolding of countless leaves,
The tinklings of thin glass in white laboratories,
Of babies' fists closed in sleep,
Of darnings and patchings, anxious breath
On window panes, infusions of tea,
Matchings of semiquavers to a ground bass,
Layings of brick on brick, scratchings of pens,
Bindings of books, drops of water over Rhayader Falls,
Of shadows hardening in cathedral closes,
Of pollen falling and drifting,
Have led to this one click of the door
As it closes behind me. And time
Begins here.

Christmas List of the Mad Musician

The complete keyboard music of Bach.
Chocolate ginger.
A knock on the door. Doesn't matter who.

Consequences

The phone call came. To make an end of it.

A voice from the darkness and the breath
As loud as the voice, and behind both breath
And voice the silly little tinkle of Sullivan,
So that, even with all wounds healed, all regrets forgotten,
There can never again be a time when the slabs
Of his stomach will not slide and his blood-hush
Fail to heat and heave at the sweet pain of
Comes a Train of
Little Ladies.

Frederick Elwell: Self Portrait

In Beverley Art Gallery

I was always more adroit with pigment
Than with people; a lost and yearning man,
But awkward in company, clumsy, tactless too,
So judged a judge by others – shallow, chill.

I seemed, I'm told, some sawdust brigadier,
Who'd bark and look askance at scruffy shoes.
This occasioned reticence, as did a certain
Stilted quality all too characteristic
Of my delicately crafted sentences,
Circumlocutory and subtly allusive,
That wove a complex syntax interlarded
Insouciantly with exotica picked up
In Paris streets. No one could believe
(I might include myself) that I could paint.

But give me a north light and a new stretched canvas,
A cool room with the Minster in the window,
My brushes tumbled in their pewter mug,
I would find myself close to tears, would feel
Again the spinning circus and the blaze
Of trumpets, sequins, swish of the trapeze;

Or swing back to Montmartre, scent again
The faint sweat of that patient naked girl
and dare to pull myself into the light;
To feel a half-intelligible world
Shake, swagger, dance along my brush
And live again and live and live again.

Never ask why I paint in a grey suit,
A shirt from Jermyn Street and a fedora.

The Considered Reply of the Mad Musician

Sir, you will have noticed that in my application
For a residency at your college I used the phrase
'Owing to' and not 'due to' which, although
Rife in even the best writing, is incorrect.
In addition, I wrote 'Were I to be offered' and not 'was I'.

I'm sorry you did not like my music, but you'll admit
I've really got grammar under my thumb.

Birthday

As easily as a newt slips into water,
As a soapy sun pulls through the scratch of cloud,
I could turn the early spring to words,

Circle the universe a few times before breakfast
Making my hay in a sweat of sun
Tried not to grasp that my days were numbered.

I wait now for the chill wind sealing the hawthorn,
The whimper of rain on dry stones.
My birthday book is full of those who died.

Memoranda for a Stonemason

I

No craft is easy, but none is as hard as this.
First you have to understand the nature
Of all that's natural. Pick out syllables
From your garrulous garden. Listen to them;
Translate. Learn their idioms.
You must teach the stone what it wants to be,
How it may shake off the world's tons,
Outflank the heavy laws of physics
And let trees crawl out into leaf, let them blossom
Where no tree can blossom.

II

Think of the stone as flesh: warm, caressable;
Or as water moved by the inaudible and invisible,
Or as winter earth in which visions may be planted.
Whatever you carve is yours; its perfection
Will remain yours alone.
But take no pride in this: so will the blame
For Jonah's misshapen nose,
That lamentable Jeremiah,
And the chipped petal of the rose.

III

Think of water falling, turning to ice in a November wind.
You are the wind and, like the wind,
Anonymous.

IV

Think of hibernation; the corolla motionless,
Tightly furled, cradled in sepals,
Asleep in the stone. The glim of a candle
Will not be enough for this awakening.
You must warm it with the traffic
Of your blood, the stonemason's palm,
The urgent, insistent breath.

V

Consider the tangible and the intangible,
The fold of leaf and the stretch of sun,
The voice and the silence,
What is and what may be.
Do not neglect laughter.

VI

To make mute stone articulate;
To stave off darkness; to shape
The single image, the unforgettable phrase
That will echo always through the rhetoric of the cathedral.

VII

Your friends coppice the hazels, mill wheat,
They mash barley, press cheeses, plough,
Or laze deep in the meadow with cows.
A few turn forests into ships; others clout
Iron flat in the bellowing forge.
Oh, easy, easy. Their world is one
Of byres, of crockery and daily bread,
Of guiding the current of what days bring;
Their dinners seldom cool on the table,
They keep their feet on the ground.
You must go beyond what's possible:
Inhabit a different time at a different pace,
Bruise and ache and bleed by choice,
Walk on air, hang in the dust-motes
With stinging eyes. Learn to love the insoluble,
The unconsenting, the repeated refusals.

VIII

Hear it first, and then
Pluck out music from the air.
It is the undershape of peony and primrose,
The lily and the crown imperial,
And the bells, all the bells
Of all our springs and summers.
Out of the earth's bone will come
The tenderness of cornstalk, tendril, fern.
Your pockets will be full of bees.

IX

Do not expect applause. Stand alone
In this tall twilight
And pull acanthus out of stone.

Through the Window

There's something wrong with this tree.
It has flu, a cold at least. Snot
Drools from a branch, then more snot;

A long string slow-motioning like paint, like glue.
Then the lament, the tree sparrows' *wheep wheep*.
A flurry then, and fling of branches; a big exit.

Not snot: albumen. At the tip of the tallest tree
A magpie bows, bows, even as his tail beats on,
Conducting the huge orchestra of sky and cloud.

Gone

No dairy. No blue milk swirling
Across the concrete.
No barn: four wet planks,
Nail-holed with orange.
Fungi. And sacks rotting.

Here and there metal
With no discernible use.

Dock. Plantain. Hogweed. Nettles.
Two steering-wheels.
A strip of harness
Hard as the earth it curls from.
The pig trough is a brandy-snap
Of rust.

A pull of regret, a ghost
Of belief in the nothing

That is left behind.

Northern Line

In the glass, too often, there are uniforms, grey, dusty,
Every station blurs them, turns them
Into what could be ghosts. So many. She looks
Through her own face into shreds of the past
Which threaten and which are vile and which are there.

She waves a hand as if dismissing a tiny piece
Of tangled air. It is an old woman's gesture
Which attracts attention only from a curious child
Whose stare, like hers, fixes on a memory,
A knot that will untangle, loosen with the day.

Faces she loved but cannot see: the musicians,
Academics, philosophers. They inhabited moments
That have become slow eternities. They shake
Under the sharp filings of the night, and a shout
Unearths a sudden scream at which she shrinks,

Presses into a corner. A long walk waits
And at the end of it a fabled feast: yesterday's bread
And a cold sausage. One bar of the electric fire
And the curtains drawn to keep the dark inside.
What can be remembered now is only the fear,

The strata under the skin, the importunities
That pushed against the will, against reason.
The ghosts warble, run against her eyes, her ears,
Waiting for what may never be spoken of until,
At last, the obituary she will never read.

Alexander: The Early Years

I pulled you, creased, from sleep; lifting you
Like a plant from its pot. When I rubbed my nose
Against your belly, your laughter as you scribbled
With your feet on my chest was half baby
And half port-soaked, middle-aged colonel
At a questionable joke.

It was a surprise to both of us; and when
I laughed, you sent my laughter back to me
With your additions, grace notes, figured bass –
Music between us: me, then you, then me.
If we are careful we can carry on like this
For as long as we live.

Not Gone

Always there are things to be remembered:
Ink-blossom, undercloud; owl-light, moth-light
And my daughter, walking alone in the headlights.
Tears sown on her cheeks by the softest of rain
And scattering, one by one, a hundred frogs.

The Cloud Shepherd

He knew them all by name. In Latin first,
As the cirrus, the cumulonimbus, nimbostratus,
Cirrostratus, altocumulus; and, when no one was listening,
As Fortune, Dido, Locksmith, Wader, Flume;
Names he used in the yard where he groomed them,
The heaps, the masses of huge air
And water deep in their deep foundations.

Out they swaggered from their pens
Into the fields of sky. He let them graze all night
Among stars and satellites, straying, clustering,
Butting the moon with their soft heads.

He had a special fondness
For the smallest of all, gusting like choirboys
In surplices. Knew how easily they could tear
On spruce, church spires, on rocky outcrops.

From their fleece he spun out scarves,
He sculpted busts of Wellington
And Bach and Vincent Price,
Stood them in cathedrals, let them melt
As the sun shouldered through. Or he wrapped
The morning crows in lacework, or flung out
A river of white stones, a city of impossible streets,
Snow caves, unskinned seashells, dunes,
Something very like a whale,
And bone-bleach and linen-fold.

And hares looked up and horses,
Towards their scud and trudge across the daylight,
While those cabined in language found ways not to see;
Ways to speak of ill winds, bad weather,
To love only the clear unending blue.

Though Yet She Speak Not

Afterwards they remembered how they had seen
Paulina (twice or thrice a day) visit that removed house;
But only afterwards, when the misery was over.

This is beyond suffering: each night haggard
With dreams that will not be shaken off, each day
Lasts more than from dawn to dark, is only ever
A crumble of twilight through long windows.

There are rules for your own good. You may walk,
But softly, and keep always to the middle of the room;
You must be mute: even a cough could betray.
No crying out, no weeping even in your sleep;
You must take care that nothing be knocked
Or overturned; no window opened; you will write no letters,
You will hear no music and will speak
Only with one woman, briefly, when she thinks it good,
And for the most part in darkness. The only sounds
You hear are the tiny ones of a world forgetting you.

Your memory alone is free to walk, but it treads
Always the same path littered with huge absences.
It will not be hard to believe that you are dead:
An ambered fly clamped in this little everywhere.

The hardest thing is to trust the plan, submit
To her refusals, her 'Not yet, not yet, not yet'
Whispered day after day.

You had heard him, your love, howl out how
He had too much believed his own suspicions.
Forgiveness ends this pain. After a fortnight. No,
Not long enough. A month? A year? Two years? Still
The whisper comes, 'Not yet, not yet.'
    You endured
For sixteen years, the trample of minute after empty minute,
Each an infinite recession of farewells.
How easy, after all, to turn yourself to stone;
Your body had only to follow your heart.

                                        But

Now you must learn to become yourself,
To wake back into flesh. What syllables
Could ever match this moment? Tell us.
Where is your tongue? Why won't you speak? Why?

Heritage

The end starts here: the finishing, the outflow. Here
Are the rejected, the broken, the corruptibles,
The small deaths for which there are no elegies.

A cracked slate, the beams dampening,
A gutter beginning to lean; and on the pergola
That rots slowly in the clay, the wires are rusting.

Tea leaves glisten – peelings, scourings, ashes,
Rinds and shells. The daily outcasts. The drain too
Is blocked and stinks, the plaster crumbles,

The door sticks. There are flies on the spoil-heap,
We walk on nothing but decay, and nothing
Will make it better. At every restoration

The cycle starts again, the rot sets in,
The sky closes, and something like night will come.

On Tour

At four pounds fifty, this Martini goes down very slowly.
Behind the bar a man flicks the television, soundlessly, from football
To a pair of lovers fighting their clothes, to a school of porpoises
Sporting off Kefalonia, to a shampoo at half price.
A woman grey-suited with red nails crosses her legs, which she wishes
were longer, fiddles with a laptop, watches the door.

Everywhere there is an air of assumed attentiveness, but each
Is alone and aware of eyes. Magazines flap; crosswords,
Menus, sudoku, catalogues are studied. Conversation happens
In whispers. A ping from the lift. Empty. A track-suited man
Strokes his belly and slumps back into soft leather, turns
His lager glass round and round; reads the beer mat. Sighs.

Two large Americans unfold a fat map and narrate their day
One to another, slightly too loudly. The drinks waiter
Engages a young woman in a conversation she does not want.
She finds herself a chair, and a book with an embossed cover
Is pulled from her huge handbag. Empty hours before dinner.
The light is fading, there is a scatter of raindrops on the glass,

And a draught from the doors; a sudden chill whiff of Bristol,
Cardiff, Nottingham, Carlisle – whatever is out there. In here
We are estranged; could be anywhere. A child shouts. Most heads
Turn. The young woman carries on reading. The lift opens,
Disgorges five men in suits who brandish briefcases, cluster
For a moment and then part. Another draught from the door.

I don't want the 'extras' on the room's television. I don't want
The room, whose key hangs behind the desk. I don't want the thick
White towels, the trouser-press, the guide to the city, the awful
Pictures above the bed, the sponge pillows, the tiny pots of milk
Or the soft biscuits. I don't want the substitute for music purring
From hidden speakers. All I want is to go home. To go back home.

Apparition

He crouches in twilight - it is always twilight here
Between two thoughts - between moon and late sun,
The garden unlatched from hours. Again he is
Dibbing, weeding, planting; always something
Slubbed with dirt that would fringe his fingernails
For days despite the bath, while ham-steam curls
From the kitchen and kale darkens in slow bubbles.

A corkscrew wind shoves the bonfire smoke
Haphazardly into the shapes of runes and sigils
Full of meaning if meaning's what I need
To glean from this land of apples, leeks and ghosts.

But there is nothing, nothing but fading light;
A comely welcome to the morning dew,
To evening frost and to the slow, sharp gleam
Of half a moon on more than half a garden.

What They Say

I don't know starvation or a bullet
In the stomach, or tented tons of snow
Crushing me off-piste. I don't know
The swift and helpless suckaway of land
As the tide-race wraps and ropes me.

I'm ignorant of shipwreck, abandonment,
Firedamp, nuclear fallout, electrocution,
Thumbscrews, the rack,
And the Chinese water torture.

Being trapped in a pothole is out of my experience,
As is swimming a sump. I've never known
My parachute not to open. Several hundred
Massive stones from cathedrals
Have failed to fall on me.

I am unacquainted with scimitars and strychnine,
Botulism and bomb-blast.

This is not even an inclusive list.

They say I should be pretty well invulnerable:
They say what you don't know can't hurt you.

The Return

Ribbons of wind beat grey from clouds,
White from the pond. Five rooks
Become twenty. Only the bomb-shelter
Where we once kept busy hens
Shields us as the air drowns in rain.

Some slates have slipped. The windows
Stare at nothing. We are out of place.

Cobbles green with last year's weeds,
The bell, tongue-tied with rust,
A see-saw tipped motionless, as if
A child had left it a minute ago,
Slid from it and gone away.

Three Watercolours for Freswick

For Murray and Monique

I

We went for an hour's walk and stood,
That afternoon, for at least a hundred years. Driftwood
Drying played reflective games with light
Beside our footprints' pressed-out semibreves.
We watched the breezes scrape the grey sea white;
Heard its India-paper rustle: prayer-book leaves
Turning and turning: an ancient liturgy for
This bridal of land and sea – hectares of both, more
Than a mind can manage. What could be
Big enough to swallow all that visibility?

Matter, spirit's bridegroom, slips a ring
On a world that's full of every single thing.

II

The sherry-coloured stairs, the whisky of the burn
That turns to Sancerre over stones, the gin-tinted sky,
All is intoxicant. We are dizzy, we sway:
Under the influence. But the castle, more hard-headed,
Stands straight, as vertical as the sea is horizontal.
It grips, as we do, an immeasurable strength.

III

Night is slow to come. The slippery moon
Makes do with what the day has left behind;
And as we sit in the flamelight and the hiss of logs,
We listen to the questions that are coming
From the curlew gargling with the last of June,
From the snipe's feathers that trip the air to woodwind.

Twelfth Night

Frost pickles the garden. Twenty cars
Queue at the rubbish tip with trailers full
Of spruce, wine bottles, paper, plastic, jars:
Off-scourings of another festival

That promised more than promise; that once more
Has failed the childlike narratives we bred
In a starlit dark, thick snow beyond the door,
And thin snow in the moonlight on the bed.

Those lucent spells are gone now with the ghosts
Of what we were. And what we are must try
To counterpoise, reclaim what entropy

Unweaves to chaos. Find the fingerposts,
The local landmarks that we steered by;
And, learning what we were, find how to be.

Appointment with Robinson

For Antony's birthday

The screen repeats its endless T-shirt joke;
Drinking water belches in its blue silo. Voices
Try it again from the rehearsal room. The paint
On the walls won't last another season,
The envelopes won't wait another day,
The telephones another minute. The copier
Opens its cyclops eye and clatters out
The first bars of *The Marriage of Figaro.*

And after daylight, every evening, comes
The shove and shatter of bottles, just at
The wrong moment, always; the mild
Terrorists with high heels and bare bellies
Going nowhere much round spilled Chinese,
Goose turds and kebab boxes; the tiny riff
Of lager cans on cobbles. Robinson
Is at the door but doesn't know the code.

And you dream again the good dream;
Words like flying fish flash past; you have,
Against the grain, against all odds,
Been dancing all day. Dancing, believing the best.

Birds and More Birds

For Andy and Sibylle

They come from somewhere else, from a hole in the sky
        That isn't there,
From out of our dimensions:
                The verger-black
  From clerestories of sycamore and maple,
      The dull-breasted hatched from bark
  Or translated, leaf to feather,
The blazing ampersands that spear the apple-bloom,
  The invisible *portamento* curling over water.

Aliens. Unaccountable.
  They hover in our air but beyond our lives;

Are gangsters clamped on the feeder,
Mice between grazing cows, crotchets
On telephone wires, cat's-cradle between hedges;
They bullet, catapult, cascade and plunge;
  They sweep and scour
        Invisible tunnels, angles of the wind
And, every time,
  Land perfectly on their shadows.

Evensong

By Purcell's grave they offered prayers for all musicians
And gave thanks for music, and for him laid flowers,
And sang 'Thou Knowest, Lord'. And then I knew
Again that he was dead, and felt the pressing absence
Of all the other dead, the known ones in the graveyard
Under willows, and the unknown whom we knew so well
And loved for their grandparenthood of all we were
And all we made, who shaped our longings, formed
A ghost of garden in our wilderness; and then
I felt words crumble and turn cold and thought I heard
The slow march of music to its own extinction,
As all the sorrow stored from great griefs and from small
Broke out its sudden unexpected anthem which was pain
And praise, was loss and gain, whose counterpoint, like his,
Untangled to the clear lightness of heart that lies below
The worst, the sour cadence that resolves. And then the silence.

Inheritance

Some mornings will tell you that it never happened,
That the rusted barn, hinge-sick and leaning
On the smoke of all your harvests, all your big horses,
Has turned to nettles at someone's garden end.

But some mornings are wrong. Listen. Your great-grandson
Is tasting the words out of your mouth, feeling
His way towards the precious places that like yours
Will be his touchstones, the measure
Of everything, under and inside and beyond.

Look in this mirror. See two people and see
The hands of a clock going one way or the other.

Horticulture and Anarchy

Between the lupins' flames, black hundreds and thousands
Suck succulence to a stick.

633 Squadron flies in from the hatchery to take out
The rocket, the green berets of lettuce.

The lawn is undermined, the rose leaves curl
Around their own death,

And roots and tubers slime round monstrous sappers,
Jointless and perfectly camouflaged.

At night the live shells on the house's hull swell, uncluster;
Grey matter in a small rain.

Our kingdom is under threat: something working,
Forever working under the skin.

Yet Another One About Spring

The old world's putting on its new disguise;
The same as last year's but we'll humour it,
Pretend delight, a dislocate surprise

At all the suddenness of greens, the lit
Lantern of the willow, daffodils
Repeating the same old song, just last year's hit

Backed once more by the hollies. Blackthorn spills
Its fooled-you frost on real frost. Spiraea
Curls and curdles, while the hawthorn fills

With mistle thrush and wren and froths like beer;
Like beer, intoxicates. Two butterflies
Try to be there as well as over here,

And we're beguiled again: all ears, all eyes.

Finale

I

We notice the weather is fine when we leave.
We don't notice the date; none of us
Keeps in our mind a sharp image of that day,
None has a memento, knows even what you wore.
Nobody told us this is what we should remember.

II

A way of simplifying yourself. No words for us,
No call to come hurrying across counties,
Only a last sleep, a drift into a new space
That had waited more than eighty years.

Rhododendrons leak light, birds are cuffed from cloud
To cloud. We watch as if it mattered.

III

'Would you like to see the body?' No.
Not white and frilled and stiff and cold.
Not with hair tidied, lipsticked, powdered; no,

But yes, if she were washing up or hanging clothes
In a blister of wind and a shower of swifts;
If she were careless of age, knitting and listening
To Haydn or Walton; making the bed, a shopping list,
A pig's ear of the crossword. Then, oh, yes,
If she were simply and deliriously awake.
    Now
We must find a slow tune for the coffin to slide through,
Words that disguise their own ineptness, some bright
Grocer's grass to hang round the surprising pit.

And then – old habit – I will watch for ghosts.